IMAGES
of America

BALDWIN PARK

Elias J. "Lucky" Baldwin was a successful businessman and entrepreneur. In 1906, it was rumored he planned to build a new town south of Vineland (the early name for Baldwin Park) and name it after himself. He was asked to visit and discuss this with D.J. Shultis, a local businessman. During the visit, Baldwin tripped and fell and was caught by Shultis's wife. He inquired what he could do in return for her saving him. They asked permission to use his name instead of Vineland, and Baldwin agreed. Shultis inscribed "Baldwin Park" on his storefront, and the village had a new name. (Courtesy of the Baldwin Park Historical Society.)

ON THE COVER: The Baldwin Park Hotel was like a home away from home. Located on Ramona Boulevard, it had a bakery for the neighborhood and a lunchroom for those who were hungry. The service was good, and customers were treated like family. The hotel rooms were comfortable and clean. (Courtesy of John M. Weis.)

IMAGES
of America

BALDWIN PARK

Robert Benbow, Lorraine O'Brien,
and the Baldwin Park Historical Society

ARCADIA
PUBLISHING

Copyright © 2011 by Robert Benbow, Lorraine O'Brien, and the Baldwin Park
Historical Society
ISBN 978-1-5316-4933-3
Published by Arcadia Publishing
Charleston, South Carolina

Library of Congress Control Number: 2010941309

For all general information, please contact Arcadia Publishing:
Telephone 843-853-2070
Fax 843-853-0044
E-mail sales@arcadiapublishing.com
For customer service and orders:
Toll-Free 1-888-313-2665

Visit us on the Internet at www.arcadiapublishing.com

Dedicated to Ria Benbow, my wife and partner,
for allowing me the time to do this book.

CONTENTS

ACKNOWLEDGMENTS

I offer the utmost gratitude and appreciation to the full- and part-time residents of the city of Baldwin Park, who have generously contributed photographs and/or information found in this book: Javier Arango, Aileen F. and Eugene Pinheiro, Manuel Carrillo, Ria Benbow, council member Monica Garcia, council member Marlen Garcia, Bruce and Trudy Garnier, Baldwin Park police chief Lili Hadsell, Grace Jordan, Bobbie and Lafe Lightfoot, Helen Merrick, Minnie Perez, Margaret Salonisen, Clint Nixon, and all members of the Baldwin Park Unified School District and the Baldwin Park Adult and Community Education Program. Thank you to all of those who enthusiastically assisted me with photographs and researched material: chief executive officer Vijay Singhai, Mayor Manuel Lozano, the Baldwin Park Woman's Club, City of Baldwin Park staff, and friends too numerous to mention.

To those in the community who have donated their time, memories, and remembrances, I salute you for these very important contributions to our history.

A special expression of appreciation and admiration goes to Lorraine O'Brien for her caring and forceful support throughout this project.

My heartfelt thanks are given to all the friends and family who offered support and patient guidance throughout this effort. I have always enjoyed history, and my love for this community has drawn me to expand my knowledge of the people that make Baldwin Park the "Hub of the San Gabriel Valley" in more ways than one.

My final expression of appreciation goes to Arcadia Publishing editor Debbie Seracini, who patiently guided me through the creation of this book.

All images used in this book are from the Baldwin Park Historical Society unless otherwise noted.

INTRODUCTION

Baldwin Park, to thee we sing our praises,
Fairest spot in all San Gabriel's vale;
Here are found all Mother Nature's graces,
Wondrous clime, where crops can never fail.
O'er thee tower beauteous purple mountains,
Shielding thee from wind and snow and cold,
Gath'ring clear, in never-failing fountains,
Water pure, transmuting soil to gold.

—Fred S. Gable

Baldwin Park dates back to 1860. At that time, Baldwin Park was part of the cattle-grazing land that belonged to the San Gabriel Mission and later to Rancho Azusa de Dalton and Rancho La Puente. Changes in ownership included first Spain and then Mexico before the United States assumed sovereign rights over the land.

With the decline of cattle ranching because of severe drought, small farmers called squatters appeared and took over the area north of present-day Ramona Boulevard. The area south of Ramona Boulevard was owned by William Workman. Elias J. "Lucky" Baldwin later obtained legal rights to this property through a business deal with Workman.

Pleasant View was the name selected by the first group of settlers in 1878. Austin Brown built the first house and dug the first well across from the Littlejohn Dairy on East Los Angeles Street. This community was composed of small farms and vineyards shaded by peppertrees. Title to this land was based on preemption and declared legally open by the federal government.

Shortage of water, then as today, was the main problem for early settlers. Farmers with no wells found it necessary to haul water from nearby wells or the San Gabriel River. Since irrigation was not used, natural rainfall was the only moisture for crops. Drought was a continuing problem with early-day residents, but between 1888 and 1891 heavy rain and winds caused great hardships.

In 1880, the name Pleasant View was changed to Vineland, with a business center around the general store at Los Angeles and La Rica Streets. The north-south streets were named Maine, Sandusky, Landis, Chicago, and Sierra Madre. The east-west streets were Clark, Los Angeles, Vineland, and Olive. Even today, some of these street names are still in use.

Between 1892 and 1895, Maine and Los Angeles Streets became the center of activity because they were on the much-traveled stagecoach line to San Jose. In 1890, the Vineland School District was formed, and the settlers constructed a two-room school building that served as a meeting place for all public gatherings and church services. Today, the Nazarene Church is now on this site.

The first church was a portable mission serving the sheepherders who tended their flocks in the foothill areas. Church services were held in the homes of local residents until the first school building was completed in 1894. Today, there are 29 churches serving the city, representing almost every religious denomination.

In 1906, Elias J. "Lucky" Baldwin, a millionaire landowner, proposed the establishment of a nearby town that was named after himself—Baldwinville. With the power and resources of a newly developed town sponsored by Baldwin, the possibility existed that Vineland could eventually disappear. To prevent this, local residents invited Baldwin, then in his 80s, to discuss his proposal at Shultis's Grocery Store. An unusual incident saved the city and changed its name to Baldwin Park. While entering the store, Baldwin slipped, falling backwards into the arms of Mrs. Shultis. A grateful Baldwin asked how he could repay being saved, and the Shultises requested the use of his name for their town. A woman's arms had saved the town, as Baldwin agreed, and Shultis painted "Baldwin Park" across the storefront.

That same year, the Baldwin Park Chamber of Commerce was organized to promote the betterment of the community. Local residents built the present chamber of commerce building in 1928. This organization has since taken an active part in all civic and economic developments of the area.

Also in 1906, the Baldwin Park Woman's Club was started and has remained active to this day. The first newspaper began in 1913, the *Baldwin Park Bulletin*. Prior to that, local news events were reported by the *Covina Argus*.

The first Boy Scout troop was organized in 1913. Women were allowed to join the chamber of commerce after its reorganization in 1913, which was a revolutionary step because the 19th Amendment was not ratified until 1920.

Baldwin Park was incorporated in January 1956 with a population of 28,056, becoming the 47th General Law City in Los Angeles County. Henry J. Littlejohn was the first mayor.

From its humble beginning, Baldwin Park now has a population of more than 70,000 and is still growing. It consists of 7.6 square miles and is a stable community. The Baldwin Park Unified School District has three high schools, four middle schools, 13 elementary schools, a children's center, a large, award-winning Adult and Community Education Program, and a district administration office. The Baldwin Park Unified School District is a highly ranked and successful educational program.

One

IN THE BEGINNING

BEFORE THE 1920S

This is the oldest map of the San Gabriel Valley. It shows the location of Baldwin Park in 1902 when it was called Vineland. There were no parklands in the mountains, only the San Gabriel Timber Land Reserve. Other cities and communities noted are Azusa, Monrovia, Glendora, Covina, Pomona, Duarte, Las Verne, and San Dimas.

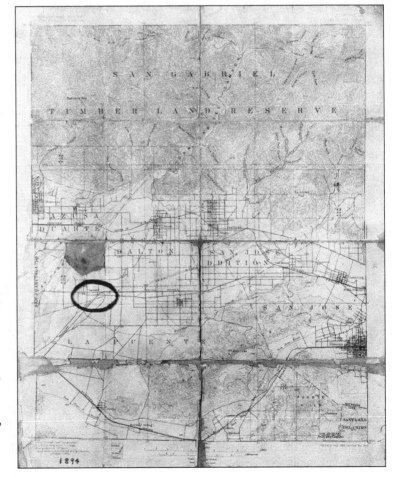

The original J.D. Shultis store was the first building to use the term "Baldwin Park." It was a general store, grocery store, and real estate and post office. In front of the store are a farmer with his horse and wagon and a lady with her child in a baby carriage. A bench on the front porch with a lady sitting on it lends a welcoming aspect. Another customer is standing on the porch posing for the picture. None of the people can be identified.

The view north from Maine Avenue in 1913 shows the Shultis Building and department store. The building on the right is still standing and in use today. The early electric poles and wiring as well as an automobile reflect the era.

Looking south from Main Avenue in 1913, one can see the furniture store on the left. It is used today as a dry goods store. The building on the right is a grocery store and has since been torn down and replaced by a two-story business structure. The Pacific Electric Trolley tracks were removed in the 1950s. Notice the period cars and the four ladies talking on the street corner.

Central School is shown under construction in 1912. It became the central school of the Baldwin Park School District. In 1936, a large auditorium with more than 600 seats was added that was used for many civic and school activities. In the background are stores along Ramona Boulevard. The streets are not paved.

This is the First Methodist Church of Baldwin Park, built in 1911. Parishioners used their famous box and pie socials to fund a new church in 1924, which was a beautiful brick building that later burned down.

This is Central School and the school park built in 1912 on property donated by Milton Kaufman. The school was for grades 1 through 8 and was part of the Baldwin Park School District. A nice park was donated in front of the school as well. This school became the first city hall of Baldwin Park in 1958, and the auditorium became a meeting place for the city for several years. After that, it became a storage facility and today is used as an art and cultural center for the city.

Mayone Mower was the first child born in the "new" community of Baldwin Park. Here she is at three years old. The Mower family has been active in Baldwin Park for years.

William and Eulala Mower are the parents of Mayone Mower. William operated the Pacific Electric Railway Red Car power station in Baldwin Park. He was a well-trained and committed employee and was involved in civic activities. The old redbrick building that housed the power station is still standing in Baldwin Park.

This 1913 picture depicts the first class at Central School. It is a combined fourth, fifth, and sixth grade, and the children seem dressed up by modern standards. The diversity of the students shows that Baldwin Park, even in those days, reflected the population that makes the city what it is today. Central School became a landmark later as the first city hall, and its auditorium was made into the city's art and cultural center.

A Central School class of seventh- and eighth-graders and their teacher, Winnefried Jeffries, are on the front steps of Central School in 1915. It must have been a cool day, as many of the students are wearing coats. One of the students, in the second row on the right, is barefoot. (Courtesy of Hessie Hoover.)

14

In 1914, one of the great floods of the area is seen at Main Avenue and Ramona Boulevard, in front of the Baldwin Park Department Store in the Shultis Building. This was before the Santa Fe Dam was built and storm drains were installed. Today there are no floods due to the Santa Fe Dam. Its recreational area provides additional parkland for the public.

One can see the damaged section of the Pacific Electric Railway (Red Car) trolley lines that were washed out in the 1914 flood. This section was between Baldwin Park and the San Gabriel River. An unidentified person is sitting on a rail, watching the water flow by. In the background are three more unidentified people: a worker, a father, and a little girl.

The rail tracks shown are on Ramona Boulevard near Main Avenue. In the background are an electric and plumbing store, a home bakery, grocery store, and automobile garage. At the far left are the Shultis Building and the old National Bank Building. There are cars parked in the middle of Ramona Boulevard near the tracks. Neither the tracks nor any of these buildings exist today.

D.J. Shultis's Baldwin Park Department Store was built in 1912 and became the main meeting place for the community. It had a department store with a horse and dog water trough located in front and metal "ring ties" to which horse teams could be hitched. The top floor was used for community meetings, banquets, and dances; and it is open, for there was no air-conditioning then. The department store drew crowds as indicated by all the cars and people.

This building represents a thriving meat market and an ice cream parlor. It was part of a business block owned by Dr. J. Locher. The meat market also sold Wilson's BBQ. There is a motorcycle in front of the stores. (Courtesy of C.L. Hollingworth family.)

Members of the Bogart family are shown in the back row with their friends, the Mowers, in the front row. These two families were very active in the early days of Baldwin Park. The sailor at left is in uniform, and Mr. Bogart in the back row wears a pocket watch. This photograph was taken before wristwatches were common.

Shown with fellow soldiers in 1918, James Jirsa is the soldier sitting on the right with his hat on. He later talked about Army procedures during the terrible flu epidemic that killed millions worldwide. He explained that they would take their bunks out into the sun every day, and those who had passed away were carried outside and cotton was used to close every orifice to keep the germs from spreading. (Courtesy of Bob and Ria Benbow.)

This shows James Jirsa as a young businessman in 1920. He ran a beer and soda shop in Cicero, Illinois. One time while delivering beer, his wife was robbed. He asked Al Capone to please stop his store from being robbed again—it never was. The Jirsas moved to Baldwin Park after World War II. (Courtesy of Bob and Ria Benbow.)

James Jirsa, Baldwin Park's last World War I veteran, is shown in his home at the age of 102. He passed away at 103. He was an active citizen in the city and was involved in veterans' organizations. He also helped start the Committee on Aging. His wife, Mae, died three years before him at the age of 97. (Courtesy of Bob and Ria Benbow.)

J.J. Rooks, pictured at the anvil, was the resident blacksmith in Baldwin Park. He is seen working with an unidentified helper while shoeing a horse. In the background are wagon wheels, a wheel fan for keeping the charcoal fire hot, and on the floor are ridges to help keep the horses from slipping. The horse is wearing a work harness for either pulling a wagon or a plow. Before tractors were available, horses did the work of moving citizens around in business and work.

William Mower is sitting and knitting in the Pacific Electric Railway power station in Baldwin Park. His job was to keep the power station working at all times. Since he had some time to himself and had to remain on-site, he learned to knit in order to stay busy and alert. There is a large turbine behind him and the control center to his left; this powered the Pacific Electric Railway trolleys.

The Pacific Electric Railway power station was constructed in 1906 and was discontinued in 1951. It still remains where it was built. It is not earthquake proof, so it has been fenced in for safety reasons. The large fans on top of the power station helped keep the turbines cool.

This two-room schoolhouse was built in 1889. The center of many community activities, it had blackboards and an outside windmill that produced water for local domestic use. This schoolhouse was later used by Japanese members of the community for educating their children about the Japanese language and culture.

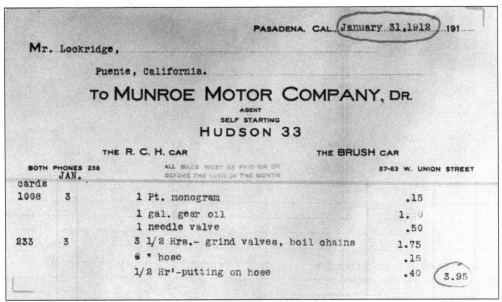

This bill reflects the reality of costs in 1912. It is for five repairs done on a car, including one half hour of labor for 40¢. The total was $3.95. Just think what it would cost today. The phone number is simply 256.

Four generations of Stowell family members have lived in Baldwin Park. The Stowells first arrived in Baldwin Park in 1913 and lived in a ranch house built in 1893 while establishing a successful orange grove. James Abner Stowell had to bring in topsoil in order to plant the orange orchard. This photograph shows Stowell (right), his son Alva (center), and his grandson Spencer. Spencer and Emmalee's son Bruce became the fourth generation of Stowells. Bruce is now a famous glass artist and successfully sells his wares worldwide. The orange grove no longer exists. (Courtesy of Javier Arango.)

This is Emmalee Stowell in front of her house that was surrounded by an orange grove at one time. She was the last Stowell to live in the house after her son left to establish his career. (Courtesy of Javier Arango.)

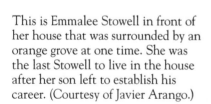

Cruz Baca was born in Mexico in 1882 and first arrived in Baldwin Park in 1906. He settled near Francisquito Avenue and farmed his own land. He gradually built his property up to 100 acres located between Ramona Boulevard and Frazier Street. Baca raised chilies, corn, yams, and tomatoes, and his cows' milk was used to produce cheese. He became the only supplier of dried chilies and cornhusks in the San Gabriel Valley. A caring, involved, and productive community member, he helped plow neighbors' fields, provided assistance and food to the needy, and was always there in times of emergency. (Courtesy of Cruz Sembello.)

Cruz Baca's and his family's involvement in the Baldwin Park community showed the positive influence that diversity can bring to an active and involved city such as Baldwin Park. (Courtesy of Ana and Humberto Montenegro.)

Susan Casas and Manuel Miranda are the maternal great-grandparents of Ana Baca Montenegro. Ana was the Baldwin Park City Treasurer for 33 years. The Bacas were one of the early families of Baldwin Park.

This is Lazaro Baca and Margarita Sanchez's matrimonial picture in front of the San Gabriel Mission in 1925. (Courtesy of Ana and Humberto Montenegro.)

Vandelia (Baca) Ruiz and her sister Ana (Baca) Montenegro are shown here in 1936. Note the car with the picture on the wheel cover that states, "Roar Gilmore." (Courtesy of Ana and Humberto Montenegro.)

This home was built in 1916 at 3004 Maine Avenue. On warm evenings in those days, people would sit on the front porch and greet neighbors walking by.

This home was built in 1914 at 4549 North Maine Avenue in Baldwin Park. Native stone has been used in the masonry.

This was the home of Margaret Heath. A school was named after her. Built in the early 1900s, this house was located at 4512 North Maine Avenue.

The old Frazier house became the Catholic convent and is in continuous use. It is located on Baldwin Park Boulevard.

The Baldwin Park Woman's Club and Baldwin Park have been intertwined from the very beginning. The club was first organized as the Vineland Friday Afternoon Club. When Baldwin Park became the name of the community, it switched to the Baldwin Park Woman's Club. The community and club both began in 1906. This present clubhouse was built in 1922. (Courtesy of the Baldwin Park Woman's Club.)

These members are receiving recognition as active members in their club. Pictured are, from left to right, (seated) Mary Dosa and Margaret Salonisen; (standing) Susan Perez, Minnie Perez, Vivian Olivas, Lea Ritter, Willa Reynolds, and Sheryl Woodward. (Courtesy of Margaret Salonisen.)

Members of the Baldwin Park Woman's Club celebrate recognition by the California Federation of Women's Club. Seen in this picture are Shigeke Stites, Joyce Gamble, and Edna White. (Courtesy of the Baldwin Park Woman's Club.)

28

Two

THE GROWING YEARS

1920s AND 1930s

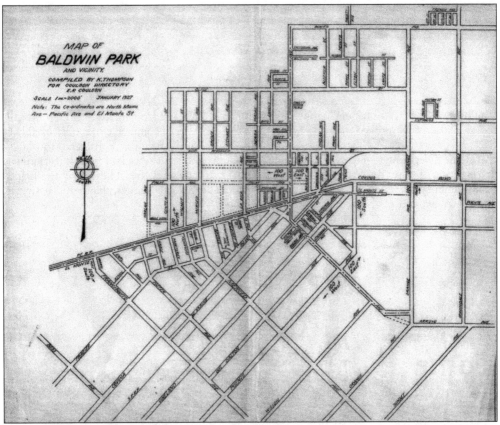

Baldwin Park was organized and laid out with well-designed streets and the Pacific Electric Railway, also called the Red Car line, along Ramona Boulevard by 1927. Since then, many streets have changed names, and more streets have been added along with shopping centers and schools. The Red Car line has closed, and the tracks were removed along Ramona Boulevard. Interstates 10 and 605 were added to make it easier to reach Baldwin Park.

The Baldwin Park Chamber of Commerce was formed in 1906 and reorganized in 1913. It was this reorganization that marked the real beginning of the chamber of commerce in modern Baldwin Park. Members discussed incorporation, domestic water rates (they were considered too high), the Home Telephone Company, the inability to obtain phones, the lack of fire protection, the preservation of water rights to the San Gabriel River, and new schools. These activities helped begin community-centered thinking that led to an increase in local business, community activities, and school expansion.

The Pacific Electric Railway line became functional in 1907 in Vineland (later Baldwin Park). It became the largest trolley line in the world. This trolley is leaving Baldwin Park and heading to Los Angeles. It is crossing over the San Gabriel River Bridge. In the background is a railroad bridge.

This picture shows Garner's meat market, located by Garner's grocery store. It was owned by ? Ganzenhuber, ? Garner, ? Rouse, and Merle Garner. Notice the old scales that were used to weigh meats in those early days. There were sanitary, glassed-in coolers for meats and cheeses.

This is Garner's market, a typical grocery store of those days. It is an open-front grocery store with an abundance of fresh fruits, nuts, and vegetables, all provided by local farmers. In those days, before supermarkets, stores kept their prices low by buying produce from local farmers and markets. Canned goods are on the back shelves, and shutters were lowered to keep the sun off the produce.

Bowman's Drug Store was set up with shelving packed with boxes and bottles of medicine and pictures for customers to purchase. The special attraction was the soda fountain on the right. There were stools to sit on and small tables with chairs. The fountain had ice cream, soda water, malts, shakes, banana splits, and more. People liked to come in to relax and enjoy the tasty offerings, and Bowman's malts and sundaes made it a very popular eatery.

Baldwin Park Community Church and Parsonage, One of the Centers of Religious Life of the Community

The Church of Christ is located at 3260 North Maine Avenue. It became the Baldwin Park Community Church and Parsonage and was one of many centers of religious life in the community. It had formerly been a Methodist church located at Ramona Boulevard and Pacific Avenue.

Juventino Miranda Sanchez arrived in Baldwin Park in 1924 and married Praxeois "Mary" Sanchez in 1936. Notice the car they are standing behind. Juventino worked for Consolidated Rock of Irwindale, a neighboring city, for many years. The Sanchezs are proud that six generations of their family have lived or are living in Baldwin Park. They are still involved in local civic activities. (Courtesy of Alice Magnusson.)

Juventino Miranda Sanchez is pictured in the 1940s as an active young man. He lived happily with his wife and family for many years in Baldwin Park. (Courtesy of Alice Magnusson.)

Pictured is a view taken from South Ramona Boulevard of the north side of Ramona Boulevard. From left to right are the Pacific Electric Railway Red Car trolley depot for Baldwin Park along the tracks, the old National Bank Building that was later torn down, and the large two-story Shultis Building at the right. In the foreground is a Baldwin Park cleaner's van of the 1929 era. (Courtesy of Rubie Kendall.)

Forest Walker came to Baldwin Park in 1910 and invested in land and farming. He owned property from Baldwin Park Boulevard to Ramona Boulevard to La Rica Street. Walker developed potato farming and later operated one of the first service stations in the community. His land was very rocky, and he leased some of it to a group of four investors to operate sand- and gravel-extraction operations. Here, he is pictured with one of his dump trucks.

34

Margaret Heath was a born teacher. In 1906, she became instructor at the old Vineland School with nine students. She was the first principal of the old Central School and won the distinction of being named Baldwin Park's first educator. When a new school was built, it was named after her, the Margaret Heath School. She retired from teaching in 1930. She also helped organize the Baldwin Park Woman's Club and the local PTA in 1918. Heath was an innovator and action taker. She passed away in 1952.

Margaret Heath (middle) is pictured with two community leaders, Marshall Lincoln (right) and Edith Lincoln. Heath was a caring and involved individual and will always be remembered.

Working on a street in Baldwin Park in the early 1920s, Charles "Bob" Ireland (second from left) stands next to an unidentified worker with an iron-wheeled pushcart, which holds road repair materials. Other workers are holding shovels, and everyone is wearing a straw hat. A dump truck sits in the background. Ireland was a member of the county road department. (Courtesy of Virginia Smith.)

This is a Hudson Touring Car that belongs to Charles and Ella Ireland. It was a popular convertible in its time. The child is Virginia Ireland, and the location is the southeast corner of Clark Street and Bogart Avenue in Baldwin Park. Interesting details in the image include the chimney on the house and the screen door to keep out insects. (Courtesy of Virginia Smith.)

Shown here is the inside of Knoll's Drug Store, which was built in the late 1920s. It was and still is located on Ramona Boulevard. A clock was mounted on the wall behind the counter, and an array of bottles, cans, and boxes of medicines could be bought. On the counter is medicine from Dr. West's for 50¢. Drugstores in those days sold all kinds of everyday needs to their customers.

Here is Knoll's Drug Store as it is today. It is now called Knoll's Prescription Pharmacy reputedly because over time the word *drug* began to have a negative meaning. In this photograph, Baldwin Park has modernized the streets with fountains and trash containers. The owners of this pharmacy do a good job helping local residents. (Courtesy of Dick Garner.)

Charles "Bob" and Ella Ireland's house at 144 Clark Street is shown here as it looked in the mid-1920s. It is a beautiful two-story home with a veranda along the front of the house with chairs on it. This was how people cooled off in those days and talked to passing neighbors. Native stones have been used on the porch, and a tree trunk has been painted white from the ground to about four feet high. (Courtesy of Virginia Smith.)

This is Harry N. Ireland's house at 202 East Clark Street in Baldwin Park in 1920. The street number today is 14606, and the street is unpaved. There are three unidentified people on the front porch and a chimney so that a fireplace could keep the house warm. Most people in those days had wood-burning stoves and or fireplaces for heat. (Courtesy of Virginia Smith.)

Here is the Margaret Heath School when it was completed in 1924. It was a primary school. This was the year that Baldwin Park's first district superintendent was chosen, J. Hampton Watts. Baldwin Park's population was growing, and the schools were overcrowded and becoming obsolete in many ways. With the leadership of the superintendent and other leaders like Margaret Heath, old schools were reorganized and new schools built. With the hiring of personnel and need for supplies, schools becoming one of the largest and most important businesses in the entire valley.

Pictured is the Margaret Heath School as it looked years later. In 1931, Margaret Heath reported that there were roughly 1,000 pubic schoolchildren consisting of about 200 in high school and 800 in lower grades. She predicted that this was a mere beginning of what the future would hold in store for Baldwin Park and its schools. Her predictions came true. Baldwin Park now has one of the most impressive and modern school districts in the San Gabriel Valley.

This 1932 photograph shows the south side of Ramona Boulevard and the entrance to Maine Avenue. The large building on the left of Maine Avenue is a combined clothing store and café. The large two-story building on the right side of Maine Avenue contains the First National Bank, Hickox Drug Store, and Mackey Hardware Store. The upstairs held the offices of lawyers and businesses. Cars of the period are parked in front. Both buildings are still in use today.

This is a group of Girl Scouts from the East San Gabriel Valley cities at a meeting in 1927. At this time, the neighborhood chairman for Baldwin Park and Bassett was Linda Hicks. There was one paid staff member, Marilyn Zimmerman, who was the field director for the council that includes 27 communities. Currently, there are about 12 Girl Scout troops and more than 200 Girl Scouts in Baldwin Park.

Baldwin Park School District superintendent J. Hampton Watts poses with the sewing class of Margaret Heath School in 1926. Learning to sew was very important during these years. This was a time before many people could just go and buy a new outfit at the store. Money was tight, and sewing was a way of life. Many people sewed or knitted all kinds of clothing items, from socks to underwear to beautiful prom dresses. Clothing items were not thrown away; they were repaired or updated.

This 37-piece orchestra represents the Baldwin Park Central School of 1926. The instructor is in the center in the second row. Notice the mixture of instruments. This is an example of the emphasis on arts at Baldwin Park schools. Baldwin Park today has some of the most impressive and competitive high school and junior high school bands in the San Gabriel Valley. They are in action at the Baldwin Park Annual Parade held in November each year.

The Baldwin Park Central School girls' basketball team is shown on the front steps of the school in 1928. Their uniforms include long hose. Girls' basketball has been around for many years. There were several successful sports programs that were active from the 1920s to today. The emphasis in team spirit, physical health, competition, and sportsmanship has been a longtime American tradition. (Courtesy of Beth Eccles Kelley.)

This fair was held annually in Baldwin Park from around 1923. A sign advertises street dances every night. The cars reflect the time period of this fair. A merry-go-round is in the distance, and there are information and fundraising booths sponsored by Pippen Furniture Company, the Odd Fellows lodge, Frostie Ice Cream Shop, Baldwin Park Lumber Yard, Vineland Acres Reality Company, a Chevrolet dealership, Irvin G. Reynolds's Buick Dealership, and Hudson Motor Cars.

Schools were where most local meetings and activities were held in the late 1930s. Here are local actors and some of the audience that attended a community drama activity in an elementary school's cafeteria. Notice the wooden chairs, the wooden plank walkway in the middle of the room, and the George Washington portrait on the wall to the left.

In 1923, Ed Roberts, Ed Tice, and Lulubelle Tice can be seen in front of their first automobile shop and garage. It was located at 3932 Baldwin Park Boulevard. The business had two gas pumps and sold Miller tires. Its phone number was 185. The driveway and street were not paved but graveled. This was one of the earliest shops of its kind in Baldwin Park.

The early 1930s showed the increasing need for automobiles and automobile repair shops. Here is E. Tice General Auto Repairing located on Ramona Boulevard. This company had a thriving business because cars and trucks were needed even though money was tight.

The Baldwin Park Savings Store had a campaign to "Come in and See one Million Dollars in Cash" to draw in customers. In front of the store is a period armored car for carrying money. With money tight, it was necessary to encourage people to save their earnings, and the bank staff hoped this would encourage people to do so and watch their savings grow.

Standing beside the Baldwin Park fire truck in 1925 is Captain Kennedy, the first fireman in the community. Sitting behind the steering wheel is Jim Taylor. This was a modern fire truck for its time and made the people of Baldwin Park feel much safer. All the other firemen in Baldwin Park were volunteers. The fire station was located on the south side of Ramona Boulevard. Behind the fire truck is a sign for a real estate and builder business.

This is the Baldwin Park Fire Department in 1932. Pictured are, from left to right, (first row) Capt. V.T. Keyes, Bob Sievenson, L.W. Jones, and Herford Epps; (second row) Captain Kennedy, Harry Critchfield, Ed Main, and Charles Tucker. Baldwin Park's fire station was located at 4213 North Maine Avenue in 1937. Station No. 29 remained at the location for 27 years before it moved to a new brick firehouse located at 14334 East Los Angeles Street. A paramedic program was started around 1969 or 1970. Baldwin Park is protected by an outstanding fire department.

Pictured is the fire department in the 1940s. Most of the firemen were volunteers who held regular practices and meetings.

Baldwin Park's first permanent home for Los Angeles County Fire Station No. 29 was completed in 1937. The station stayed there for 27 years, then moved to a new brick fire station at 14334 East Los Angeles Street and is still there today.

Shown here are fire engine 29 and the unidentified firehouse dog. The Dalmatian is known as the standard fire department dog.

Webster's Refuse Disposal picked up trash in the San Gabriel Valley from 1931. Owned by the Otting family from 1948, Webster's served the residences, industries, and commercial customers in Baldwin Park for years. Today, Webster's has been replaced by Waste Management Company.

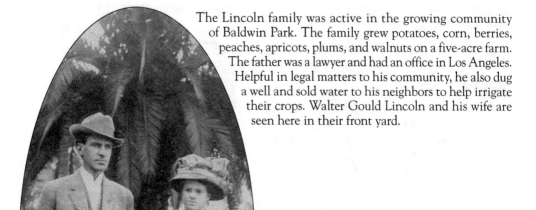

The Lincoln family was active in the growing community of Baldwin Park. The family grew potatoes, corn, berries, peaches, apricots, plums, and walnuts on a five-acre farm. The father was a lawyer and had an office in Los Angeles. Helpful in legal matters to his community, he also dug a well and sold water to his neighbors to help irrigate their crops. Walter Gould Lincoln and his wife are seen here in their front yard.

The Lincoln family drilled a well and set up a water pump and cistern. Lincoln also sold water to his neighbors for their use and for irrigating their farmland. Marshall (left) and Allen Lincoln stand on the water tower. The height of the cistern was beneficial for increasing water pressure.

48

Smith's Furniture Exchange shows
how businesses adjusted during the
Great Depression. Trade and barter
was used almost as much as cash. It
worked well, as money was in short
supply. People sometimes traded their
labor for items that they needed.
(Courtesy of Isabel Christie.)

Ramona Boulevard had one of the
earliest washing machine repair shops
and electronics stores in the area. It
sold new and used washing machines,
radios, and other electronic items.
Repair and resale was very important
to the success of the store in those
days. (Courtesy of Isabel Christie.)

The Barnes Circus Winter Quarters were in Baldwin Park for several years. Today's Barnes Avenue and Barnes Park are in remembrance of this era. This elephant is hauling away timber from a walnut grove that is being demolished. On January 24, 1976, Dolly Jacobs, who trained the Barnes Circus elephants, came to Morgan Park in Baldwin Park and talked about her experiences. She brought an elephant named Jewell for the annual parade.

The Al G. Barnes Circus went the way of other small traveling circuses of the era. This shows what one of its trailers looked like. The wagon itself weighs 5 tons and is capable of carrying a 10-ton load. Each of the massive wheels weighs 500 pounds. This vehicle is one of more than 100 circus wagons that can be seen at the Circus World Museum in Baraboo, Wisconsin.

This old icehouse was located on East Pacific Avenue in Baldwin Park. The Baldwin Park Ice Company controlled the icehouse until the demand declined and it was no longer profitable. The structure has been torn down, and a residence is now located at the site.

"Dutch" Manning is pictured with his dump truck. Manning hauled sand, gravel, and other materials in the 1930s and had a profitable business. There is another truck and a trailer behind the vehicle he is posing in. Baldwin Park had a great deal of gravel and sand, which made these types of business so successful.

This old Central School orchestra is reflective of the time. In 1935, a Mr. Manning directed this group. Pictured are, from left to right, (first row) Malcolm Lincoln, Jenell Allen, ? Manning, Mildred ?, Douglas Bryant, and Onesa ?; (second row) Newell Fields, Jimmie Taylor, and Don Root. This group had four brass pieces, two woodwinds, and two violins.

These gentlemen were instrumental in setting up a new subdivision in what was, in 1933, an unincorporated area. It was built along Maine Avenue and became part of the Baldwin Park community.

This communication from the Los Angeles County superintendent of schools to Charles D. Jones, superintendent of Baldwin Park city schools, states that Vineland School District came into existence on May 7, 1888, and was later made the district of Baldwin Park on August 10, 1914. The first trustee election was held in Vineland School District on June 4, 1888. At that time, the following trustees were elected: Andrew Cole, George Sells, and M.S. Wilson.

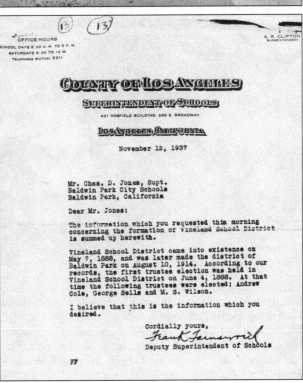

Along with the farms in Baldwin Park came the development of dairies. One of the earliest dairies belonged to the McMullens. This picture shows the "original family" milking cows by hand. It was very hard work to milk so many cows, and it was typical for hands to cramp and become sore. Running a dairy was never-ending but profitable work. Cows generally needed to be milked twice a day and fed, the stalls needed to be cleaned, and the milk and cream had to be sold, among other chores. (Courtesy of the McMullen family.)

Joseph McMullen is outside his milk barn showing off his milk cows that were kept in cattle pens for feeding. He had different breeds of cattle to produce large amounts of creamy, mild milk. The McMullens sold their dairy to John and Julia Dospital in 1924. Hoof-and-mouth disease struck the cattle in the 1920s, and they had to be destroyed. The McMullens set up another dairy and had to destroy their cattle due to hoof-and-mouth disease in the 1930s. They held onto the land until 1965. (Courtesy of the McMullen family.)

The community of Baldwin Park needed recreation space for the growing community. In 1931, J.W. Morgan sold what was formerly an orange grove at a large discount because he felt that the youth of Baldwin Park could use it for wholesome recreation. Here, surveyors are in front of their old van displaying their equipment used to survey the land and mark out the Morgan Park area. The men are wearing high-top leather leggings.

The large steam shovel and dump truck were used to dig and move the excess earth to other locations. There was a large amount of sand and rocks to move to create holes for wading pools and an especially deep hole for the outdoor swimming pool called "the plunge." These machines were modern for the 1930s.

This is the audience for the grand opening of Morgan Park. Notice the old wooden chairs and the hats worn by both men and women. The shrubbery had just been planted. To the right are two men leaning on a piano that was brought for the grand opening.

A great many people showed up for the grand opening of Morgan Park. The shrubbery is freshly planted, and banners fly on poles in the background. Some of the early businesses of the time can be seen, and a long line of cars shows how many people attended for the grand opening. The three sailors by the cars are wearing their dress whites with bell-bottom trousers. Behind the cars is Ramona Boulevard.

Carnival action is shown at the grand opening of the park. Some park equipment is visible, and in the background is a large ladder used by high divers to dive into a water container. There are slides, small merry-go-rounds, and a small boy in a cowboy uniform in the foreground. Over the Morgan Park building in the left background looms the tower of the Mormon tabernacle. It was later purchased and torn down as part of a large expansion to Morgan Park.

The opening of "the plunge" was a special event because locals could swim in a pool instead of the river or local ponds. The plunge was designed with two shallow ends and a deeper section in the middle. Youth are lined up on the diving board, and swimmers are wearing Morgan Park's all-wool bathing suits.

Beauty queens from surrounding areas and cities were part of the entertainment. Standing from left to right are Miss Monrovia, Miss Monte RV Park, Miss Temple City, and Miss Baldwin Park. They were greeters and part of the welcoming committee.

This is the 1921 graduating class of the Baldwin Park Central School. The teacher was Margaret Heath; she is fourth from the left in the back row. Heath later had a school named after her. From left to right are (first row) Ed Mulrooney, Robert "Jake" Rooks, Peter Ciaccio, Leslie Garner, Donald Scott, Lester Jensen, Earl Starr, and Elmer Tannler; (second row) Christine Wahl, Louise Jensen, Marian Holbrook, Margaret Heath, Gertrude Ganzenhuber, unidentified, Tessie Pavelko, Mabel Kempson, Mildred Stols, Helen Johnson, and Teresina Roggero. (Courtesy of Donald Scott and Lou Lochridge.)

This shows a gathering of the Baldwin Park Rotary Club in 1933. Many of the men have hats and wear the stylish "drape" type of pants and suits. There is only one woman present. The flags are symbolic of all the countries that have Rotary Clubs. (Courtesy of the Baldwin Park Rotary Club.)

Three

BEING DISCOVERED

1940s

This is an aerial picture of the intersection of Ramona Boulevard and Main Avenue taken in 1945. The Pacific Electric Railway trolley lines are in the middle of Ramona Avenue; they were replaced in the 1950s. Many businesses lined the north side of Ramona Boulevard. The vacant lot on North Maine Avenue and Ramona Boulevard became a service station, and today it is a hamburger stand.

This monument is in honor of those from Baldwin Park who served in the armed forces. More than 1,200 young people from the community served in World War II. All veterans from various wars are recognized by Veterans Day ceremonies and in the Baldwin Park Anniversary Parade.

The Baldwin Park Chamber of Commerce's minutes from May 19, 1913, contain an excerpt that mentions a discussion about establishing a Boy Scout troop in Baldwin Park with the chamber of commerce backing it. There is some confusion as to whether a troop was begun. Another Scout troop was started in 1923. Frank Barnato started a club sponsored by Margaret Heath School in 1942. This shows a parade with the Odd Fellows sponsoring both Boy and Girl Scouts in the trailer.

This picture was taken on December 19, 1941. It shows the air-raid wardens for Baldwin Park. Their job was to help people obey the special emergency laws of these early days of World War II. Men, women, and some children wear their air-warden hats, which were World War I helmets. Behind the air-raid wardens are the military vehicles and trailers along with some Red Cross support vehicles. (Courtesy of Mack and Clara Green.)

Lillian Mower felt that she was born to be a member of the military. She tried to join the Navy and failed because she did not meet the weight requirement. The Coast Guard did not demand that a person weigh as much. After eating bananas and other types of food, she made the weight and became a SPAR (from the Coast Guard motto Semper Paratus, "Always Ready"), the name for the women's corps. She trained and became a driver and radio communications person. Stationed in Hawaii, Mower volunteered in the amputee ward of the base hospital. She also helped entertain soldiers.

Lillian Mower played the accordion and did dances and sung songs for the soldiers. Here, she plays her accordion and entertains several soldiers and sailors in Hawaii. Mower came from a military family. She had members who served in the Revolutionary War and Civil War and a son that served in special Air Force units until he retired. She still does not rest, as she is an active member of the Baldwin Park Woman's club.

Clyde Slagowski flew in bombers during World War II. He was both lucky and unlucky. He was shot down in North Africa in 1943 and captured by Germans and put into a prisoner-of-war camp in northeastern Germany. He was a POW until 1945. Slagowski was freed and returned safely home to America. He was a gunner and is shown here in his flying outfit carrying a .30-caliber machine gun. (Courtesy of the Slagowski family.)

Crew of the "Bad Penny," 398th Bomb Group, early 1944

JOHN RYAN
1st Pilot

ROY TEST
Co-Pilot

CARL FOSTER
Navigator

DAN DAME
Bombardier

LLOYD STOVALL
Radio Operator

JOHN COWLEY
Flight Engineer/
Top Turret

FRANK COOMBS
Ball Turret

RAY KEENE
Tail Gunner

SAM DEVAN
Waist Gunner

Roy Test was one of Baldwin Park's local World War II heroes. He is seen standing in the back row, second from the left (with the circle around his head). This bomber was named *Bad Penny*, and the crew is pictured here all together. Roy flew 35 missions and remained involved with veterans groups. He received many special awards and recognitions for his activities, attended congressional ceremonies, and was active in the community of Baldwin Park. He passed away in December 2009. He will be missed. (Courtesy of Irene Test.)

This photograph shows Roy Test and his wife, Irene, in civilian clothes. In between Roy and Irene is Bob Benbow. Roy was very involved in the city and in the Adult and Community Education Program. He and his wife were members of the adult school community advisory committee and other city committees. They were honored for their efforts. (Courtesy of Irene Test.)

Eugene A. Pinheiro was stationed with the US Army Air Force in Assam, India, from 1944 to 1945. This shows him smoking a cigar and relaxing in a homemade chair sitting by a bunk with string webbing. The soldiers lived in tents. When Pinheiro returned, he married and became a schoolteacher in the Baldwin Park Unified School District until he retired. He was a very involved leader in the Baldwin Park Historical Society for many years. (Courtesy of Eugene Pinheiro.)

Marcelo Sanchez (left) was in the 101st Airborne Division in World War II. He is Ana Montenegro's uncle and a native of Baldwin Park. Sanchez was wounded in five places and captured by German soldiers. This picture shows Marcelo in his airborne uniform before parachuting into France. He is standing at attention, and to his right is a well-known figure, British prime minister Winston Churchill. He is inspecting Sanchez and his jumping gear. (Courtesy of the Montenegro family.)

This is a picture of Marcelo Sanchez in a 101st Airborne Division uniform. He was a World War II hero—he suffered five wounds and became a prisoner of war in Germany for 11 months. (Courtesy of the Montenegro family.)

Ralph Guerra Baca was in the US Army in World War II when he was called upon to serve in 1944. The Baca family has been part of Baldwin Park since 1906. They are still very active in civic activities. (Courtesy of Cruz Sembello.)

Harold and Mina work in their victory garden in their backyard. During the stress of World War II, many Americans started victory gardens to help reduce the need for rationing and to provide fruits and vegetables for their tables. Growing these gardens helped minimize the concern about producing food supplies for the country's 16.6 million people in the military. Victory gardens also provided good morale for American citizens. The fenced-in structure behind the garden in this photograph is a henhouse.

Kenneth and Nina Burnham were master weavers and loom builders. They were involved in building, selling, and weaving from the 1930s. Kenneth designed and created many types and sizes of weaving looms. A special one he developed in the 1940s was for paraplegics. This was necessary due to so many wounded servicemen and servicewomen. They could make all the motions to operate the looms with only their hands. Nina designed and created different patterns of threading for many companies and home designers.

During the days of World War II, the nation's railroads reached a new peak of proficiency. Railroad companies had to be sure to deliver military goods and supplies of all types in a timely manner so they could be shipped to the proper military units in different locations and theaters. The main type of locomotive used at the beginning of the war was a coal-burning steam locomotive, which could be spotted by its plumes of black smoke. Towards the end of the war, train companies developed the first diesel locomotives. They were able to push and pull heavier loads than steam locomotives and did not cause as much pollution in the countryside. Diesel engines were cheaper to run, and after the war they slowly replaced the steam locomotives. By the 1960s, it was very unusual to see a steam locomotive.

The Baca family has been an involved part of Baldwin Park since 1906. This is a photograph of Cruz and Juanita Baca (elderly couple in the center of the first row) and family in 1949. There are 35 family members in this picture. Standing on the far right is Ana Baca Montenegro, a teacher who also served as Baldwin Park city clerk for 33 years. (Courtesy of Cruz Sembello.)

D.J. Shultis poses with his wife, Eugenia, daughter Josephine Shultis Sawyer, and granddaughter Susan. This picture was taken in the 1940s when Baldwin Park was being discovered by the many people who moved to California or were temporarily transferred there during the war. Many people liked the climate and either remained or later moved back. This caused another big jump in the population of Baldwin Park.

PHOTO -- GEORGE SCOTT

The Shultis Building was originally a grocery store. In those days dogs ran free in the streets, and local farmers drove their wagons, pulled by horses, to the grocery store to sell various fruits and vegetables to the owners. To make the farmers feel more welcome and because he liked animals, Shultis had a dog and horse water trough put in front of his store. Several metal rings to which horses could be tied were implanted in the concrete.

Pictured here is an early-1940s parade in Baldwin Park. The parade route in those days was along Ramona Boulevard and up North Maine Avenue. A farmer is driving a tractor and pulling a trailer that has two boys and several clowns; no one is identified. Their float has a Western motif. In the background are cars and horsemen riding the parade route.

Looking east on Ramona Boulevard, cars and people line the street to view the parade. There are a Ford four-wheel tractor, horsemen, and ladies moving along the parade route. In the background is Knoll's Drug Store on the left and Morgan Park on the right. The Red Car trolley tracks are still located in the middle of Ramona Boulevard.

Ray Blaylock wears a Roy Rogers–style hat and cowboy belt buckle that highlight his Western style. He is standing on a cement sidewalk near the entry door to the Social Club, where locals played snooker, ate hamburgers, and drank coffee. An advertisement in the window reads, "Drink Sparkeeta, a Sparkletts 'up' drink."

This is the staff of Jones Junior High School in 1949. In the group are many successful teachers and future administrative leaders in the Baldwin Park Unified School District. One of the strengths of the district was the promotion of individuals from the teaching ranks to administrative positions. They were proven leaders who knew the community and the limitless possibilities of their students and staffs. (Courtesy of Aileen Pinhiro.)

The Steel Furniture Manufacturing Company was started in Baldwin Park in 1927. It was not until the late 1940s (after World War II) that steel furniture took off. The Steel Furniture Company was in the right position at the right time and produced excellent furniture for many years. The leaders of the company also became involved in the community of Baldwin Park and helped it become a city.

Four

THE CITY BEGINS
1950s

This picture shows a portion of the growing business sections off North Maine Avenue and Ramona Boulevard. In the middle of the street is the Pacific Electric Railway's Red Car track. To the left on the northern side of Ramona Boulevard are a Shell service station, a café and bar, Merits Loan Shop, a music center, Three Pigs Café, and a Firestone tire shop. On the right-hand side of Maine Avenue is Crawley Men's Wear store, a drugstore, and the Market Basket combined market. Three unidentified businessmen are holding a discussion on the corner of South Maine Avenue, and the period cars define the time frame of the image.

Wally's Bike Shop was a well-known store located on the south side of Ramona Boulevard for years. Wally serviced and sold new and rebuilt bikes and was also a much-needed locksmith and lock salesman. He was involved in training young men in bike repair skills and was well liked by the community. Two unidentified girls ride a tandem bike in front of the store, whose variety of bikes sold can be seen through the windows.

The Bank of America had a ground-breaking ceremony on North Maine Avenue in 1950. Present are various representatives from Bank of America and Baldwin Park Chamber of Commerce. Baldwin Park started a serious advertising effort to draw attention to the open areas and rapid growth of business in the soon-to-be city. The city started the Hospitality Hostess program in order to welcome people to the community and to make people aware of the city. The chamber of commerce assisted in this effort.

An active chamber of commerce holds its installation dinner in 1955. This gathering was held at Baldwin Park School District's Charles Jones School. The school cafeteria was decorated with artwork and displays made for and by the children.

Isabel Christie taught dancing for 45 years, and the Isabel Studio Swim School opened in 1960. These are young ballerinas performing at the old Central School auditorium. Christie held shows several times a year.

These young bunnies were trained by Isabel Christie. They are performing on the old Central School auditorium stage. She had a large studio and swimming pool located on La Rica Street. Christie produced several stars: one became the Los Angeles Dodgers' organist at the age of 16, a young man became a United Service Organizations (USO) presenter in the Korean War, and she trained a swimmer who placed in the top 25 in 11 events in the United States in 1980.

This is an early graduating class of eighth-graders. The ceremony was held on the old Morgan Park lawn. Wooden chairs that are still being used in the 1950s, and families are standing in the background.

The old Central School building became the city hall for the young city of Baldwin Park in 1957–1958. The structure had been refurbished and updated to better meet the city's needs. In 1978, the city staff moved into the new civic center building and saw the old city hall torn down.

This photograph shows the location of the Baldwin Park police headquarters in 1956. It was in the basement of the old Central School, which later became Baldwin Park's first city hall. A civilian and police officer (both unidentified) are in the basement as the offices are being worked on.

In February 1956, Helmer "Pat" Syhre, a 57-year-old retired veteran of the Los Angeles Police Department, was hired as acting police chief of Baldwin Park's new police department. Eighteen officers were sworn in by city clerk Elmer Cook. They began patrol on the night of June 30, 1956. Syhre brought the tan uniform of the highway patrol to Baldwin Park as the standard uniform. (Courtesy of the Baldwin Park Police Department.)

Baldwin Park police chief Helmer "Pat" Syhre (right) talks to an unidentified officer next to one of the new police cars of the time. The uniforms are tan with a black tie, and the emblem of the "Hub of Baldwin Park" on the car door.

In the late 1950s and early 1960s, worry about the growing smog problem in Los Angeles County increased. A concern was that people using old incinerators, found in nearly every backyard, contributed to smog. Two unidentified Baldwin Park policemen inspect an incinerator that needs to be dismantled. Notice the motorcycle officer is wearing a black bow tie. (Courtesy of Catherine Bloxhem.)

The Baldwin Park police patrol is lined up for inspection in 1958 or 1959. Members are standing against the old Central School auditorium, located behind the old city hall and the new civic center. Dressed in civilian clothes, Baldwin Park police chief Louis Torres (1957–1961) is the second person from the right. A police motorcycle is front and center, ready for inspection.

The Baldwin Park Police Department brought on its first female officer in 1975. Kim Plates was hired for office work but began going on patrol immediately. She is the officer in the middle. The other two department personnel are unidentified.

In this 1973 photograph are officer John Cisneros and Dutch, the department's first police dog.

Baldwin Park police chief Lili Hadsell is the first female police chief hired by the City of Baldwin Park. In 1999, she began her career in Baldwin Park as a police lieutenant. In 2006, she was assigned to the Support Services/ Professional Standards Bureau as the bureau commander. For personal growth, she attended the FBI National Academy. On May 4, 2008, she was appointed chief of police of the Baldwin Park Police Department. In 2010, Hadsell was named Woman of Distinction 2010 by Congresswoman Judy Chu. (Courtesy of the Baldwin Park Police Department.)

The Baldwin Park Police Department of today has different uniforms than the ones worn in the 1950s. These officers are being introduced to the public at a meeting in the civic center council room. They are handsome men and women in their uniforms. (Courtesy of the City of Baldwin Park.)

Pictured here is a new 2010 Baldwin Park Police Department squad car. The "Hub of the San Gabriel Valley" emblem is no longer on the side doors; instead, they proudly read "Baldwin Park Police." The city's black-and-whites equal the most modern police cars available at the time. (Courtesy of the City of Baldwin Park.)

The Baldwin Park Police Department has four motorcycle police officers. Here, they ride in the Baldwin Park Day Parade. Baldwin Park had just won the honorific title "Playful City USA" for its outstanding parks and recreation programs and areas. (Courtesy of the City of Baldwin Park.)

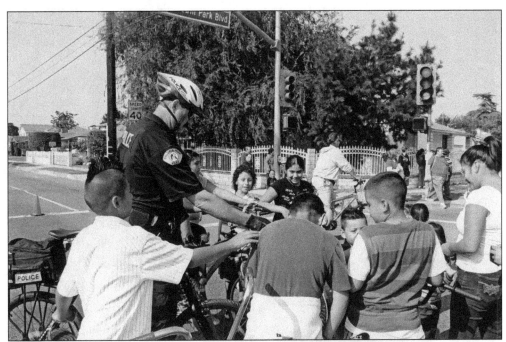

In an attempt to show the full outreach of the Baldwin Park Police Department and its close relationship with the community, the department has instituted bicycle police. They are quiet and can show up anyplace anytime. They help bring things up close and personal. Children talk with an unidentified bicycle officer in this picture. (Courtesy of the City of Baldwin Park.)

Baldwin Park continued to grow, and water is always a key factor in a city's growth. Shown here is the 1950s ground-breaking for the city's new reservoir. From left to right are businessman and city councilman Lynn Cole, water district member Roy Judd, and Don Holmes, who was involved with the Baldwin Park County Water District and many other civic affairs.

The Baldwin Park Rotary Club sponsored this float in a Baldwin Park parade. The gentleman in the passenger seat of the Jeep is holding a gun of some sort. An insurance business and the Baldwin Park Medical Clinic can be seen in the background. (Courtesy of the Baldwin Park Rotary Club.)

This Red Car trolley with Baldwin Park on its destination marquee was the last passenger trolley car in Baldwin Park. The first trolley started on July 4, 1907, and the last one operated on October 14, 1950. This last car was celebrated with people waving good-bye, a blazing red traffic flare or two atop the rails, a farewell clang, and a whistle toot—and the 43-year-old era of trolley cars was over in Baldwin Park. Many people wish the trolley-car era had never ended.

The Littlejohn Dairy was opened in 1944 by Henry Littlejohn and his father. Littlejohn Dairy served local people and all the local schools from 1947 to 1973, when the business closed down. It sold pasteurized milk that came from three kinds of cows: Jerseys and Guernseys gave richness to the milk, and Holsteins provided quality.

This is the Baldwin Park Lions Club float for the Baldwin Park Christmas Parade in 1951. Baldwin Park had many service clubs that were active in the community. Proud Lions Club members are gathered around the parade float they all helped to create. A Christmas elf sits inside the logo. (Courtesy of Bob Brodsky.)

This large mobile home park called Baldy View Trailer Park was purchased in 1959 by Mark and Lorraine O'Brien. It met the housing needs of many people from the 1940s to the 1980s. Initially, it had a large area for the plant workers and farmworkers who moved in and out during the war years, then it became a place for gypsies to winter in the 1960s. After it was purchased by the O'Briens, there were strict regulations for those who stayed there. It was sold to the City of Baldwin Park in 1989 and awaits redevelopment as of early 2011. (Courtesy of Lorraine O'Brien.)

The original Cole's Market started on the east side of Pacific Avenue. In the 1940s, it outgrew its first location, and a larger store with an added liquor section was built across the street. Lynn Cole (left) and W.R. "Wimpy" Cole were the co-owners. The store has changed proprietorship but is still called Cole's Market. An active member of the community, Cole belonged to the chamber of commerce, city council, and other boards and service clubs over the years.

The chamber of commerce continued to provide leadership for the city with its involved business membership. This is a typical business luncheon held in the old chamber of commerce building in November 1951. Those in attendance were chamber board members.

Pictured is a Baldwin Park parade in the 1950s. It shows a large Cub Scout Pack No. 65 marching down the street. In the background is old Morgan Park. This was the time when the parade route was along Ramona Boulevard to North Maine Avenue. One of the Cub Scouts is proudly leading the pack while holding the American flag.

This photograph shows the Baldwin Park marching squad leading a parade while carrying letters that spell the city's name. A large crowd is gathered on both sides of the street to watch. To the right of Ramona Boulevard are the Chamber of Commerce Building and different businesses. It looks like a cloudy day for the parade.

Humberto "Monte" and Anna Baca Montenegro are active members of the community. Anna was a schoolteacher and joined many Baldwin Park organizations. She was city treasurer for a record 33 years. Her husband was a US Marine during the Korean War in the 1950s. He started an electrical company that is still going strong. Monte says his business keeps him young. Pictured is Monte in his Marine dress uniform when he first entered the corps in 1953. (Courtesy of the Montenegro family.)

Five

TAKE US TO THE FUTURE
1960S AND 1970S

In 1973, Baldwin Park instituted a minibus service in order to assist the elderly, handicapped, and other individuals. At the ribbon-cutting ceremony for the opening of this highly desirable support service are, from left to right, Emmit Waldo, Donald Holmes, Councilman Leo King, Miss Baldwin Park, unidentified, Councilwoman Adeline Gregory, and unidentified. This was the beginning of a much-needed service to help citizens get around.

Robert "Bob" and Julia McNeill (above, second row, fourth and fifth from left) and family settled in Baldwin Park in 1964. Bob was an active citizen of the community. He became a member and leader of the Baldwin Park Host Lions Club, Boys Club, and the Manpower Consortium. Bob worked in the Los Angeles County Assessor's Office and became a councilman of Baldwin Park in 1978. Julia was a cardiovascular tech at the USC Medical Center and a member of the Baldwin Park Woman's Club and other groups. She became a councilwoman after Bob passed away. Their nine children have been highly successful; they are involved in law firms, professional sports, education, religion, real estate, and high-tech businesses. The family members continue a tradition of positive support of community wherever they live. (Courtesy of the McNeill family.)

From left to right are Chief Dale Adams (1965–1976), Officer Cliff French, Officer Don French, and Councilwoman Adelina Gregory. This photograph was taken in 1975 to show the receipt of a grant for traffic safety programs.

The Baldwin Park Community Hospital was the city's first hospital. The small facility built in the 1960s at Francisquito and Puente Avenues served its patients well.

The new Baldwin Park City Civic Center is seen still under construction on July 8, 1978, its day of dedication. The beautiful and well-designed building is in use today.

Here is the Baldwin Park Civic Center as it looks today. It has heavy traffic from citizens and features a large council chamber. The chamber allows many participants to hear the council meetings and speak and ask questions. It has really opened the meetings to all citizens.

Ladies in Baldwin Park take part in the early polio prevention clinics of the 1960s. They are waiting for their shots. This helped many people stay healthy and not be affected by the terrible disease.

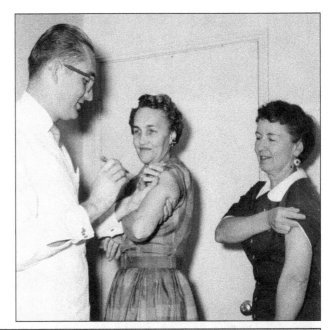

Pictured is the grand opening of Baldwin Park's new and expanded civic enter. In attendance were the local congressional representative, state senator, city council members, and mayor. It was a proud moment for Baldwin Park. Pictured are, from left to right, city council members Robert McNeill, Bob Izell, and Felipe Aguilar; John Rousselot, congressman; Joe Montoya, state senator; Jack White, mayor pro tem; Russell Blewett, mayor; and Richard Cunningham, project coordinator.

The clock tower of the old Baldwin Park High School is shown here in the 1970s. The door under the tower was where the early Baldwin Park Unified School District Adult School had its office in the 1950s and 1960s. It was called the Baldwin Park Evening High School in those days. Today, the Baldwin Park Unified School District has award-winning Adult and Community Education School programs open all over the city from Mondays through Saturdays in mornings, afternoons, and evenings.

The main campus of the Adult and Community Education School is located at 4640 North Maine Avenue and is called the BPACE Center. It is set up like a small community college and has classes such as basic skills and English as a second language as well as vocational training programs. Childcare is provided for students. There are many sites that make up the Baldwin Park Unified School District's (BPUSD) adult supportive services for career, social, and community education. This is a photograph of the entrance to the BPUSD Adult and Community Education Center.

This is the performing arts center for the BPACE Center. Completed in 1990, it is used by the city, district, and other community organizations for meetings, shows, performances, and various activities. The center has a stage and fly gallery and can support bands, plays, and other entertainment as well as public meetings. It has been used as a cultural exchange site, has a yearly Chinese New Year program, and can be leased for uses as approved by the Baldwin Park Unified School District School Board.

The Baldwin Park Chamber of Commerce is a center for local businesses. Pictured are community leaders Don Holmes (left) and councilman Virgil Hamilton (center) having a "race" to kick off new businesses. Frank Kihm (right) is ready to start the action with a pistol. This photograph was taken in 1977 as the town's industries expanded. (Courtesy of Baldwin Park Chamber of Commerce.)

Supervisor Pete Schabarum is seen here in 1977 with Baldwin Park officials at the dedication ceremony of the Santa Fe Dam Recreation Center. This opened a beautiful and much-needed place for people to relax and enjoy themselves. From left to right are unidentified, Councilman Felipe Aguilar Jr., unidentified, Pete Schabarum, Mayor Emmitt R. Waldo, and two unidentified.

In the late 1960s, Baldwin Park still had a business like Via's Turkey Farm. Customers could buy broad-breasted turkeys for special meals and holidays. The farm also had a petting farm that schoolchildren visited to learn about various animals and actually see them and touch them.

The service clubs of the city helped defer the costs of this sign that was installed on the corner of Ramona Boulevard and Maine Avenue in 1968. Active members of the city and the Rotary Club enjoy the view. From left to right are unidentified, Mayor Joseph McCaren, and Henry Littlejohn, the first mayor of Baldwin Park. (Courtesy of the *San Gabriel Valley Tribune*.)

A new post office at 4230 North Maine Avenue was completed in 1960. After changing location many times over the years, the post office found a permanent home in the $205,000 structure. In 2011, it continues to serve the community from this facility. This is a photograph of the ground-breaking ceremony for the building.

The Baldwin Park Chamber of Commerce holds a grand opening for Citizens National Bank in January 1961. The bank opened on the southwest corner of Ramona Boulevard and South Maine Avenue in a two-story building constructed some time earlier. The only recognizable face in the ceremony is Councilman Lynn Cole, standing to the right of the bow in the ribbon.

This is the grand opening of Charlene's Hair Design Beauty Salon. It was a new enterprise in the ever-growing Baldwin Park business community that was located on North Maine Avenue. The people's hair and clothing styles are typical of those in a c. 1965 image.

Royal Coaches began in Baldwin Park in 1973 and has grown consistently. The body shop and towing business was founded by Roberto and Lilia Salazar. Their four children run the daily operations of the company. Recently, it won a Small Business of the Year award from Assemblyman Ed Hernandez of the 57th Assembly District. Royal Coaches has its own tow trucks and automobile bodywork. One of the activities that the business accomplished has been to actively seek out ways to make life better for the people in the community.

Gov. Ronald Reagan (second from left) visits local resident Al Rubio of 3944 Stichmore Street in the 1960s. He is seen with, from left to right, Betty Browning, Danny Villanueva, Gordon Browning, Al Rubio, and unidentified. He visited the city during his term as governor of California. It was a proud day for Baldwin Park to have Reagan visit.

Six

City on the Move
1980s to Present

Bruce Jacobson has been a State Farm Insurance agent since 1980. He is a Vietnam War veteran and is still a member of the US Coast Guard Auxiliary. Jacobson has been involved with the chamber of commerce, Boys and Girls Club, Rotary Club, and has been a semiprofessional magician and entertainer over the years. He is the owner of this State Farm Insurance company in Baldwin Park.

In the 1980s, members of the Baldwin Park Host Lions Club are seen receiving charity donations to help those who are blind or need glasses. From left to right are Lions Club president Bob Benbow, councilman and Lions Club member Bob McNeill, ? De Dios, and councilman and Lions Club member Felipe Aguilar Jr. (Courtesy of the Baldwin Park Host Lions Club.)

In the early 1980s, the Baldwin Park Unified School District Adult and Community Education Program began a teen parent program to encourage teen parents to provide quality care for their children and help them complete their schooling. This van was donated to help pick up teen mothers and their children and take them to class. Adults in attendance in the early 1990s are Mayor Fidel Vargas, teacher Pat Brown, school superintendent Larry Kemper, school board member Ralph Nunez, and an administrator from the adult school. (Courtesy of the Baldwin Park Unified School District.)

Jack Tanaka was not only an instructor for the Baldwin Park Unified School District Adult and Community Education Program but was an artist in his own right. He taught all aspects of ceramic production—art, creativity, design, and baking—and ran the ceramic center for the adult school. Tanaka was the department head of the ceramic program for years.

This is a working lunch meeting of the Baldwin Park Chamber of Commerce in the 1980s. Gathered around the table are community leaders. The chamber was a driving force behind bringing businesses to Baldwin Park. During the 1980s, there were more than 700 businesses that became members of the chamber of commerce.

Seymour Holtzman, executive director of the Baldwin Park Chamber of Commerce, was just what was needed in the city. He was the executive director for many years and became the sparkplug that reinvigorated the chamber and kept it going for his tenure. He was a friend to both Baldwin Park and its businesses.

Lee and Sandy Lucas were very involved in Baldwin Park. Lee was the Los Angeles County parks person who took care of Morgan Park. When the city took over its parks, Lee became the director of human services and was involved in the birth and direction of Baldwin Park's park and recreation division. Lee was named Outstanding Professional by the Los Angeles County Basin Parks and Recreation Association.

Manuel and Vera Rocha were Baldwin
Park residents and active in the Shoshone
people's cause. Vera was the local chief,
and Manuel was the local spiritual leader.
They were present at the El Pueblo
State Historic Park in Los Angeles for
the April 1986 ceremony that formally
recognized the Gabrielino Nation.
Vera became chief in 1991. Most of the
Native American display was donated
by her or the San Gabriel Mission.

In the 1980s, Baldwin Park began persuading more businesses to become part of the community.
One of the ways this happened was this sign mounted on Ramona Boulevard in 1985. This action
and other ideas by the mayor and city council brought in many new businesses.

In 1925, several small independent water companies combined and incorporated as the Baldwin Park County Water District. The Valley County Water District serves portions of the communities of Azusa, Baldwin Park, Irwindale, and West Covina. This company responds positively to community input and proudly shows its name and emblem on one of its large water tanks that is located on Baldwin Park Boulevard and Arrow Highway.

In 1948, a dream became a reality in Baldwin Park. Harry and Esther Snyder opened their first In-N-Out Burger restaurant at the corner of Francisquito and Garvey Avenues. The first drive-thru in California, it was a success from the start. This shows the construction of In-N-Out Burger's store No. 1 in 1948. At the time, the roads were poorly paved, and the area was not crowded. (Courtesy of In-N-Out Burger.)

Here is a memorable photograph of In-N-Out Burger's store No. 1, open for business in 1948. Notice the cars. (Courtesy of In-N-Out Burger.)

This aerial view shows In-N-Out-Burger store No. 1 as it appeared in the early 1950s. At the time, the business was in a rural setting. (Courtesy of In-N-Out Burger.)

Harry Snyder was a family man. Here, he is with his wife, Esther, and their sons, Guy (right) and Rich, at the first In-N-Out Burger store. The boys are wearing captain's hats and sitting in a period speedboat. (Courtesy of In-N-Out Burger.)

Esther Snyder was a caring and community-oriented lady. Here, she is with her two sons, Guy (right) and Rich (left). Esther was active in Baldwin Park, where she was on the board of directors of the Boys and Girls Club and was effective in helping Morgan Park take its first step to becoming the award-winning park it is today. (Courtesy of In-N-Out Burger.)

Harry Snyder's business philosophy was simple, "Give the customer the freshest quality foods you can buy and provide them with friendly service in a sparkling clean environment." When the construction of the I-10 Freeway caused store No. 1 to close, a second In-N-Out Burger was completed on Francisquito Avenue. As In-N-Out Burger grew, it developed new methods to ensure quality, cleanliness, and service remained the top goal. The first In-N-Out Burger corporate office was developed in 1981. To assure the quality standards remained the same at all new locations, a training system was developed for managers and staff. The First In-N-Out University was completed in 1992, and now there is a second In-N-Out University due to expansion. By 1985, the restaurant had 40 locations. (Courtesy of In-N-Out Burger.)

This is an oil painting of Harry Snyder that hangs in In-N-Out Burger's Baldwin Park headquarters. It is a reminder that his philosophy is still the driving force that guides the successful In-N-Out Burger organization. (Courtesy of In-N-Our Burger.)

This oil painting of Esther Snyder shows her during a period of leadership and successful development of In-N-Out Burger. She was a loved figure in Baldwin Park and was involved in some of the positive changes as reflected today. (Courtesy of In-N-Out Burger.)

This shows the second generation of leaders in this family-owned business. On the left is Rich Snyder and on the right is Guy Snyder. They successfully led In-N-Out Burger to an expansion that today numbers 258 locations in four states. (Courtesy of In-N-Out Burger.)

Residents of Baldwin Park are proud of their city. Here is Sgt. Everett N. Marquez of the US Marine Corps as he shows the world where he comes from by hanging the flag of Baldwin Park from a building in Fallujah, Iraq. It is people like Marquez who help make Americans' freedom possible, and he represents the youth of this country at their best. (Courtesy of the Everett Nickolas Marquez family.)

This is Army Sgt. Joe Gallegos (left) of Baldwin Park holding a Baldwin Park city flag while stationed in Baghdad, Iraq. The photograph was taken under the victory arch that Saddam Hussein built to celebrate one of his wars. (Courtesy of the Joe Gallegos family.)

The civic auditorium (the former Central School auditorium) was built in 1936 and opened in 1937. It was designed to seat 750 people. The auditorium was used by the Baldwin Park School District until 1954, when it was then decided that another Central School should be built at another location. In 1958, the City of Baldwin Park bought the old Central School for its first city hall and the old Central School auditorium for a meeting place.

This is a picture of the old Baldwin Park City Hall and its council meeting room. It was terribly small and so crowded that meetings with large attendance had to move to the old Central School auditorium. From left to right are Councilman Joseph McCarron, Councilman Ivory Crites, Mayor Charles Morehead, Councilwoman Adelina Gregory, and Councilman William Adair.

The old Central School auditorium was refurbished and opened to the public in 2007. It was changed and updated to become the Baldwin Park Arts and Recreation Center (ARC) and holds art exhibits and classes for the community. The facility became the permanent home for the Baldwin Park Historical Society and the Baldwin Park Historical Museum. The museum has displays from the beginnings of Baldwin Park to the present. It provides research facilities and has a Hall of Heroes for those who have served in the military.

This mural was developed by the art class of the school district's Baldwin Park Adult and Community Education Program. It was installed as part of the Baldwin Park Historical Society's donation to the hallway wall on the ground floor of the civic center between the council meeting hall and the police department center. It was created in 2005 and reflects the various influences that made Baldwin Park what it is today.

The department of recreation and community services has successfully accomplished many projects over the past decade. It has been presented with several awards in recognition of its extraordinary achievements and services provided to the community. Pictured is the Hilda L. Solis Park, which was dedicated to former Congresswoman Solis in 2003 after the opening of the adjacent teen center and skate park. The park was later modified to include an outdoor fitness zone with multiuse equipment. (Courtesy of the City of Baldwin Park.)

The teen center and skate park opened in 2003 after Baldwin Park received designated state funding. The facility was the first Healthy Teen Center in the San Gabriel Valley. It offered healthy snack and beverage options in all of its vending machines. It has added additional fitness and health benefit areas. (Courtesy of the City of Baldwin Park.)

The Esther Snyder Community Center opened in 1990 and was named after Esther Snyder, the cofounder of In-N-Out Burger. Over the years, the facility has expanded to include an indoor aquatic center, a day care for the East Valley Boys and Girls Club, and the administrative headquarters of the department of recreation and community services. Among the many awards won by the department of recreation and community services are the 2009 and 2010 Playful City USA awards from KaBOOM!, an organization that promotes recreation areas for American children. (Courtesy of the City of Baldwin Park.)

The Baldwin Park Aquatic Center was built in 1990 and features an indoor pool. The facility is connected to the Esther Snyder Community Center and was constructed on the site of an old outdoor pool that was built in the late 1930s. "The plunge," as the earlier pool was called, drew crowds of all ages that flocked there to enjoy a cool swim and escape from the scorching sun. (Courtesy of the City of Baldwin Park.)

The Julia McNeill Senior Center was renovated in 2007 as one direct response to the increasing needs of seniors in the community, in particular the baby-boomer population. The renovation and expansion included a designated library, a television room, meeting rooms, and office space to accommodate the growing population of seniors. McNeill was a former city council member. (Courtesy of the City of Baldwin Park.)

The Teri G. Muse Family Services Center was the original center for Baldwin Park senior citizens, but it outgrew this facility. The family service center was reopened after a small expansion in 2005. It is home to multiple service agencies including Goodwill, Kaiser Permanente, and MAPS 4 College. The parks department has won awards for Barnes Park, its ARC Single Focus brochure, the teen center and skate park, and its summer activities. (Courtesy of the City of Baldwin Park.)

Waste Management, located at Stewart and Live Oak Streets, has proudly served the Baldwin Park community for more than 40 years. There are 140 employees at the Baldwin Park facility. Thirty-nine employees and their families have been long-term residents of Baldwin Park. Waste Management is committed to being a strong community citizen and is proud of its involvement as an active partner to the City of Baldwin Park. It works with nonprofit sectors in many ways to help the economic climate. (Courtesy of Baldwin Park Waste Management.)

Baldwin Park mayor Manuel Lozano is the longest-serving mayor since the city's incorporation. He has been in office since 1999 and is serving his sixth term. During his tenure, he has been proactive in drawing businesses to Baldwin Park. Lozano was interviewed on the CBS *Evening News* after Baldwin Park passed a moratorium prohibiting any new drive-thru restaurants for a 45-day period as the city conducted a study to determine the negative health impacts of such restaurants. (Courtesy of the City of Baldwin Park.)

The Baldwin Park County Water District built its district office in the 1980s. It is still there, and the water is as good as ever.

This was one of the city's first shopping centers. The Alpha Beta grocery store brought a new and larger market to Ramona Boulevard.

Baldwin Park has always had open and active parade participation over the years. It is a reflection of the citizens' beliefs in the community and the nation. This float shows how schoolchildren believe "The Best is Yet To Come" not only for them but also for their community and schools.

This float shows a combination of the successful East Valley Boys and Girls Club and the Baldwin Park Judo Club, which teaches self-reliance and self-defense. Both organizations strive to build strong boys and girls who can handle life's challenges and to teach them to be self-confident and become good citizens.

This float representing Baldwin Park Christian School indicates another strength of the community. This truly American city has an open and honest approach to life. It helps diversity become strength. Baldwin Park's long history is part of what brings the whole community closer. This is reflected in the many successful city and school district programs.

This is the celebration of the opening of the permanent home of the Baldwin Park Historical Society's museum. Picture are, from left to right, Councilwoman Marlene Garcia, president and museum curator Robert "Bob" Benbow, and Baldwin Park mayor Manuel Lozano. The year 2007 was a good one for Baldwin Park. It won the Arts and Recreation Center Facility Design award from the California Parks and Recreation Society. The old Central School auditorium was reopened for the residents of the city to enjoy.

This is a large political gathering held in Morgan Park to welcome Arkansas governor Bill Clinton during his 1992 campaign for US president. He was welcomed by a large crowd and the mayor of Baldwin Park, Fidel Vargas (1992–1997). It was the first time a candidate visited Baldwin Park during a presidential campaign.

Fidel Vargas, former mayor of Baldwin Park, brought fame to the city in 1994, when he was recognized by *Time* magazine as one of 50 national movers and shakers under the age of 40. He was elected mayor of Baldwin Park at the age of 23. This made him among the youngest mayors in the United States. During Vargas's tenure, Bill Clinton, governor of Arkansas and presidential candidate at the time, came to Baldwin Park for a campaign visit. (Courtesy of the Fidel Vargas family.)

Fidel and Margarita Vargas moved to Baldwin Park in 1978. They raised eight children who attended several Baldwin Park Unified School District schools as well as Saint John the Baptist School. Fidel was a carpenter, and Margarita was a school-community liaison. Their eldest son, also named Fidel, was elected mayor of Baldwin Park, and their youngest daughter, Teresa, was elected to the Baldwin Park Unified School District board. Margarita was elected to the Valley County Water District Board. (Courtesy of the Fidel Vargas family.)

Kaiser Permanente was formed during the Great Depression and World War II. Henry J. Kaiser, an industrialist, and Sidney R. Garfield, a surgeon, pioneered an integrated, prevention-based medical-care program that has changed the face of health care. It is one of the nation's largest nonprofit health plans, serving 8.6 million members. Kaiser Permanente has a long history of in the San Gabriel Valley that began almost 50 years ago. The first medical office building was opened in West Covina in 1963. This vacant drive-in was purchased by Kaiser Permanente, which built a large medical center to serve the East San Gabriel Valley at the site. (Courtesy of Kaiser Permanente.)

Kaiser Permanente has opened other medical offices all over the San Gabriel Valley in places like Diamond Bar, Industry, Montebello, Baldwin Park, San Dimas, and Pasadena. When construction of the Baldwin Park Medical Center was completed in 1994, it served members on an outpatient basis only. By 1998, it formally opened as a hospital and now serves more than 230,000 members. The medical center offers a wide range of services, including inpatient and outpatient care along with state-of-the-art birthing suites. Here, it is pictured under construction. (Courtesy of Kaiser Permanente.)

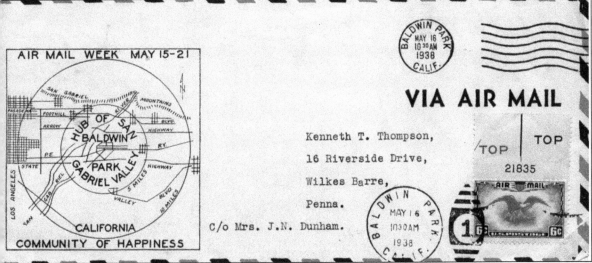

This interesting air mail envelope from 1938 shows that Baldwin Park, "the Hub of the San Gabriel Valley," was known as a California Community of Happiness—and it still is. With its people, schools, organizations, and churches, Baldwin Park is a city whose residents enjoy where they are today. They look forward to where they will be in the future.

Visit us at
arcadiapublishing.com